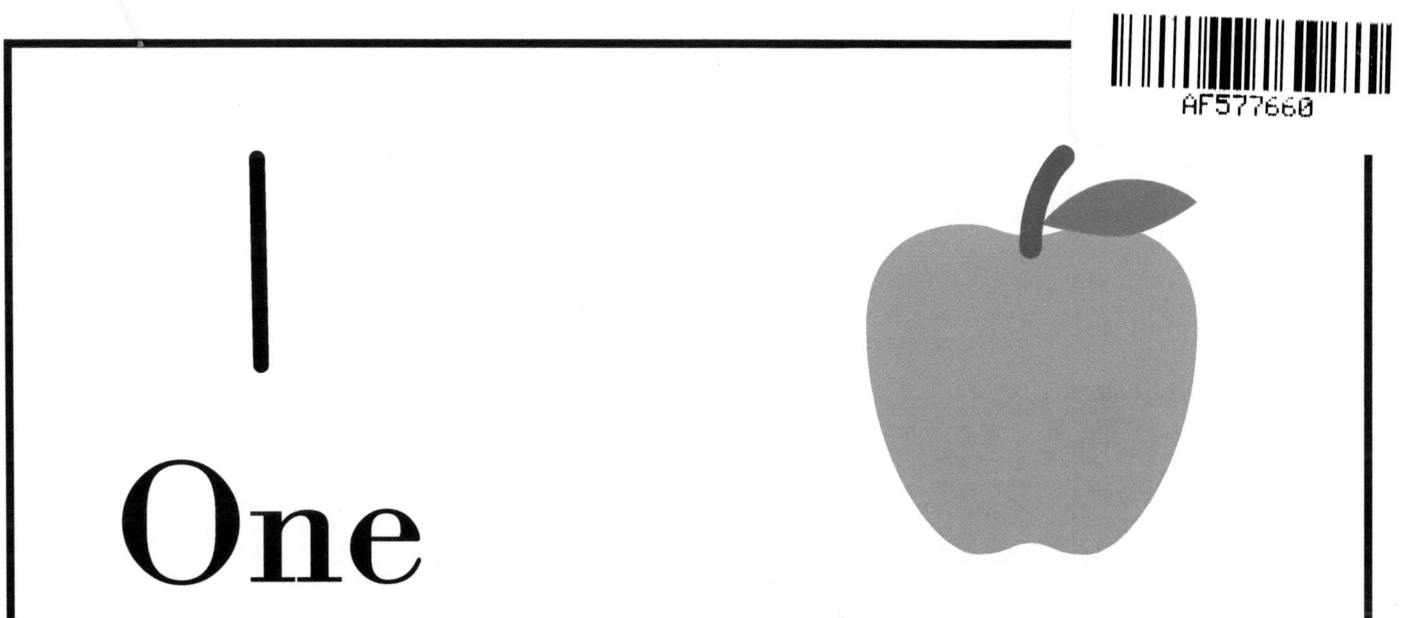

SAY, TRACE AND WRITE

1

1

1

1

SAY AND WRITE

I

2

Two

SAY, TRACE AND WRITE

2 2 2 2 2

2 2 2 2 2

2 2 2 2 2

2 2 2 2 2

SAY AND WRITE

2 2 2 2 2

3

Three

SAY, TRACE AND WRITE

3 3 3 3 3

3 3 3 3 3

3 3 3 3 3

3 3 3 3 3

SAY AND WRITE

3 3 3 3 3

4

Four

SAY, TRACE AND WRITE

4

4

4

4

SAY AND WRITE

4 4 4 4 4

5

Five

SAY, TRACE AND WRITE

5 5 5 5 5

5 5 5 5 5

5 5 5 5 5

5 5 5 5 5

SAY AND WRITE

5 5 5 5 5

COUNT, SAY AND WRITE THE NUMBER IN THE BOX

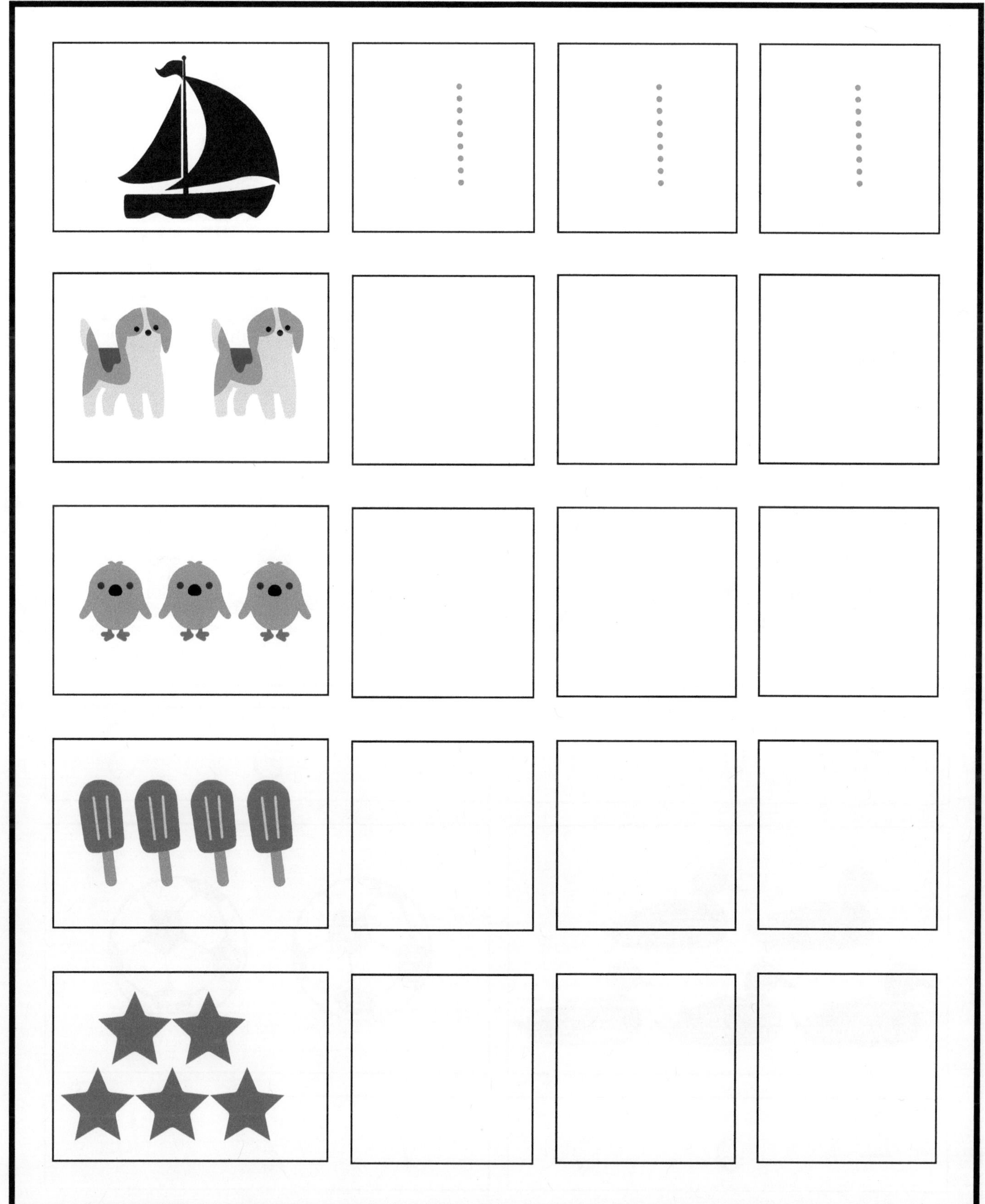

COUNT AND CIRCLE THE CORRECT NUMBER

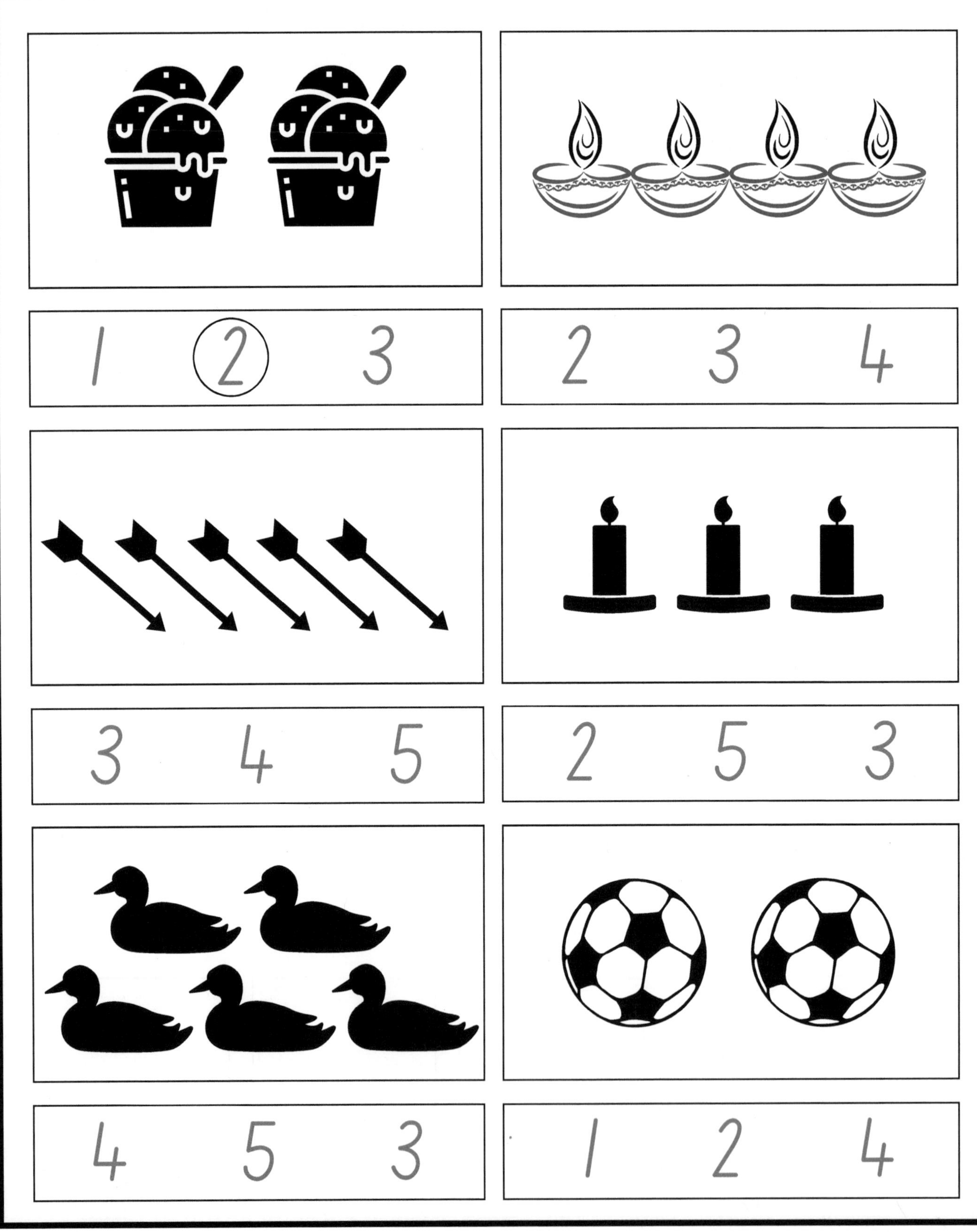

6

Six

SAY, TRACE AND WRITE

6 6 6 6 6

6 6 6 6 6

6 6 6 6 6

6 6 6 6 6

SAY AND WRITE

6 6 6 6 6

7

Seven

SAY, TRACE AND WRITE

7

7

7

7

SAY AND WRITE

7 7 7 7 7

8

Eight

SAY, TRACE AND WRITE

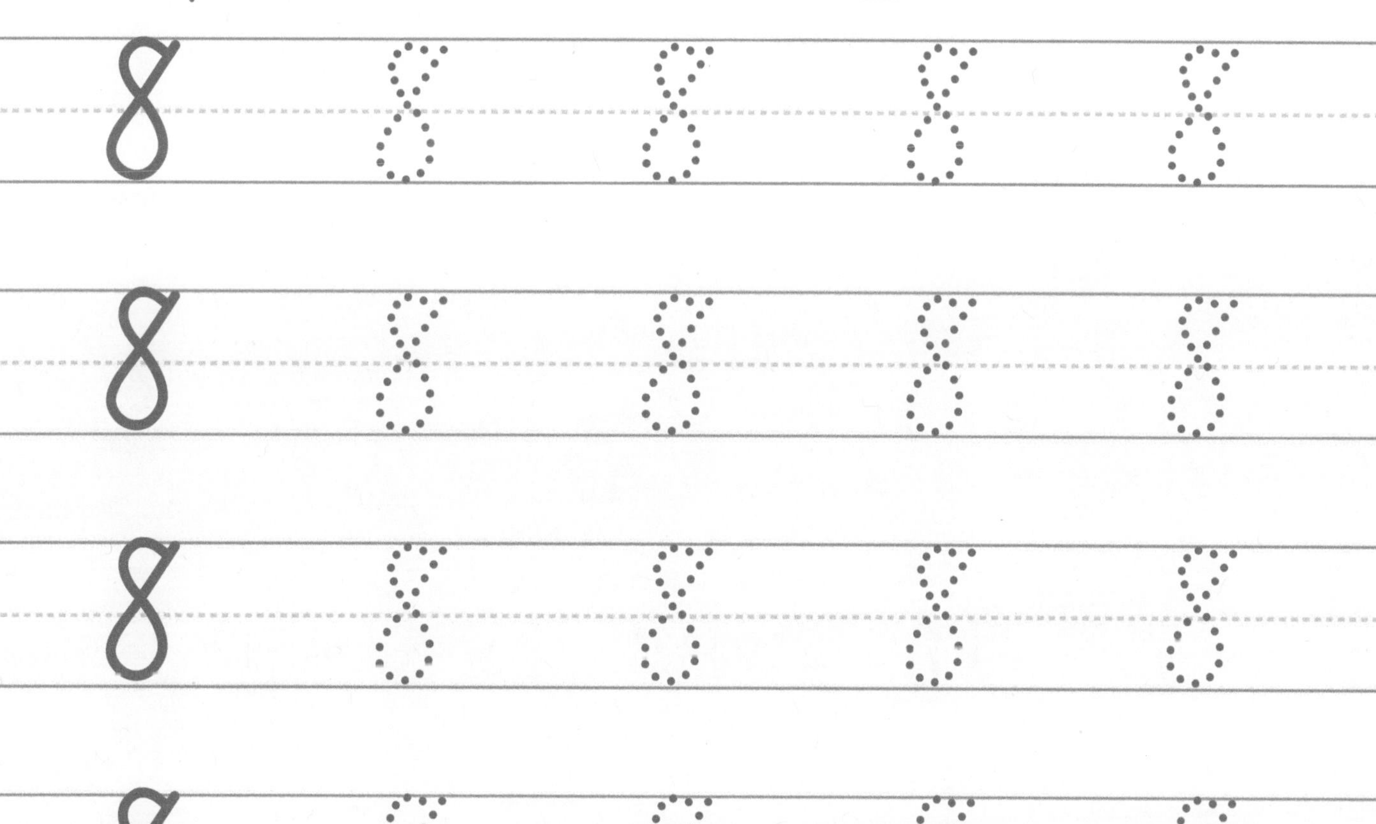

SAY AND WRITE

8 8 8 8 8

9

Nine

SAY, TRACE AND WRITE

9

9

9

9

SAY AND WRITE

9 9 9 9 9

10

Ten

SAY, TRACE AND WRITE

10 10 10 10 10

10 10 10 10 10

10 10 10 10 10

10 10 10 10 10

SAY AND WRITE

10 10 10 10 10

COUNT, SAY AND WRITE THE NUMBER IN THE BOX

COUNT AND CIRCLE THE CORRECT NUMBER

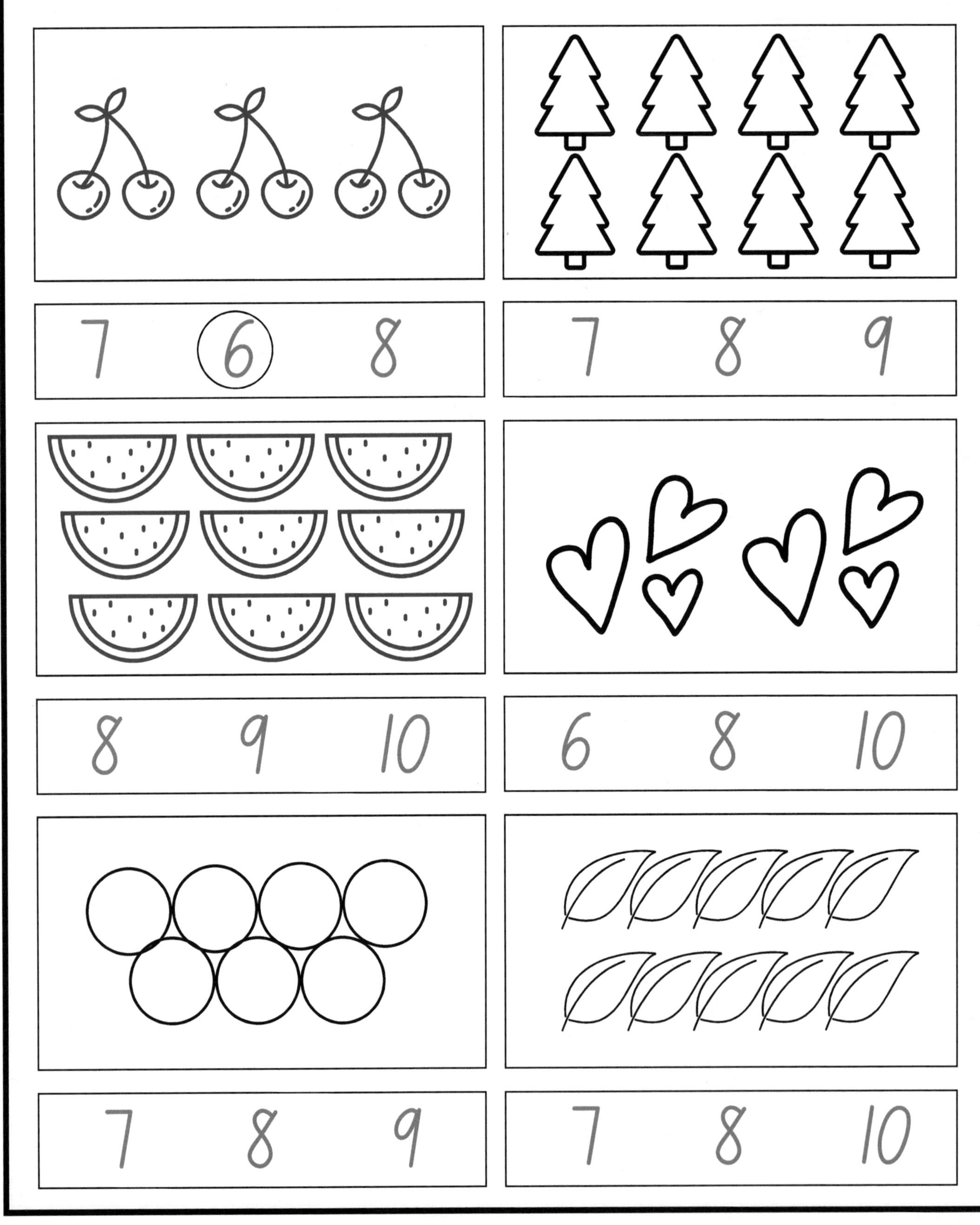

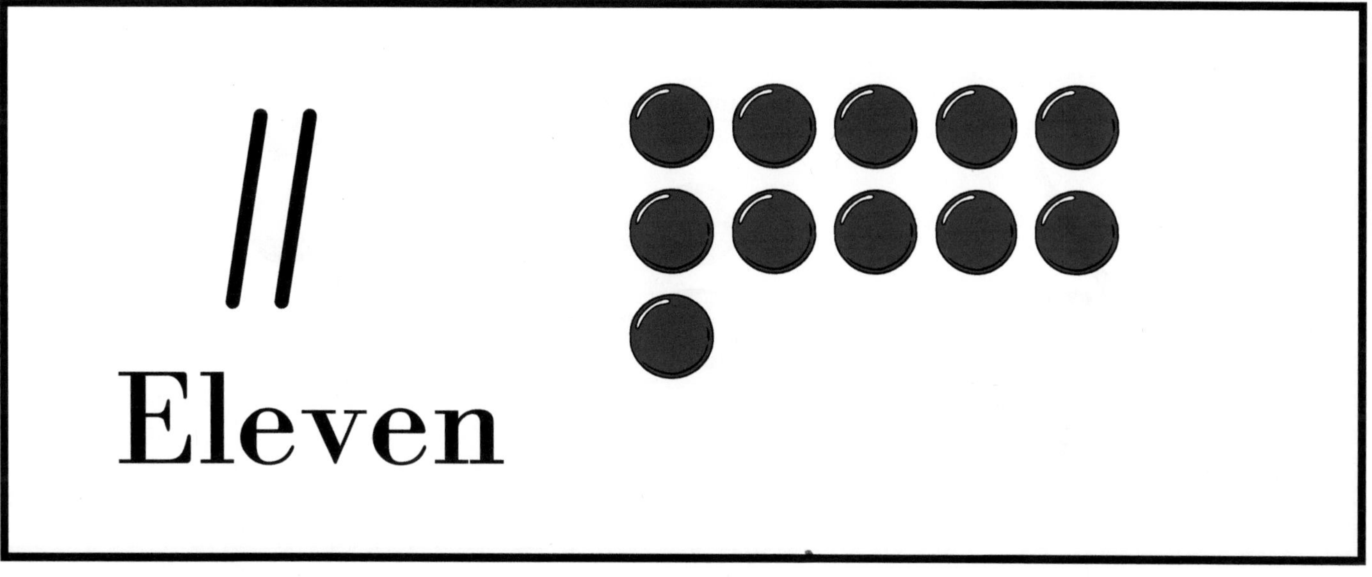

SAY, TRACE AND WRITE

11 11 11 11 11

11

11

11

11

12

Twelve

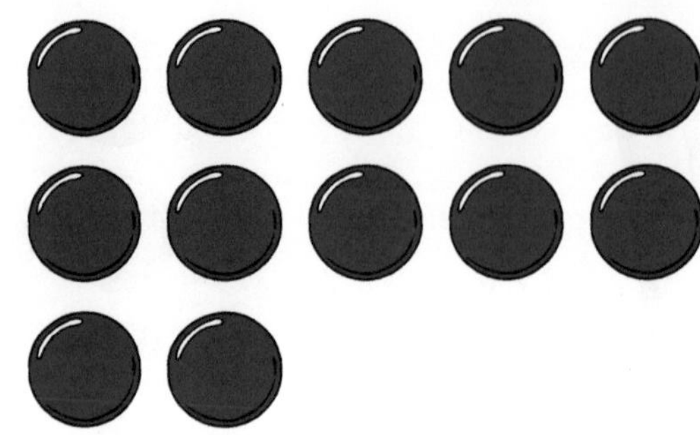

SAY, TRACE AND WRITE

12 12 12 12 12

12

12

12

12

13

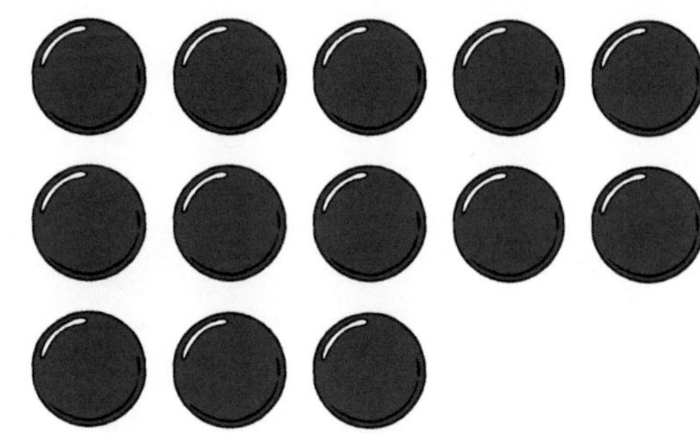

Thirteen

SAY, TRACE AND WRITE

13 13 13 13 13

13

13

13

13

14

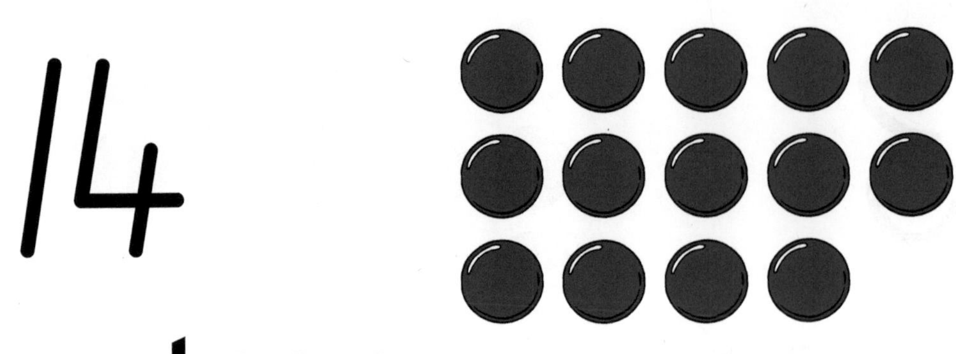

Fourteen

SAY, TRACE AND WRITE

14 14 14 14 14

14

14

14

14

15

Fifteen

SAY, TRACE AND WRITE

15 15 15 15 15

15

15

15

15

WRITE THE NUMBERS FROM 11 TO 15

11					
12					
13					
14					
15					

COUNT AND CIRCLE THE CORRECT NUMBER

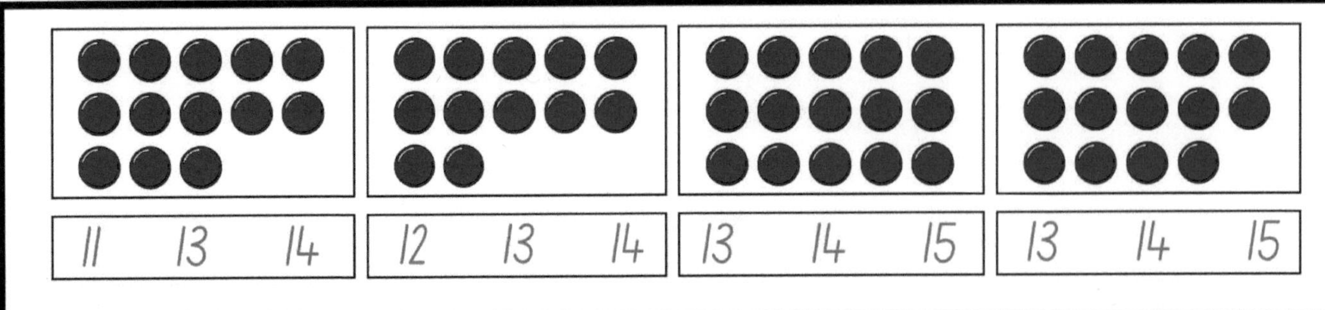

16

Sixteen

SAY, TRACE AND WRITE

16 16 16 16 16

16

16

16

16

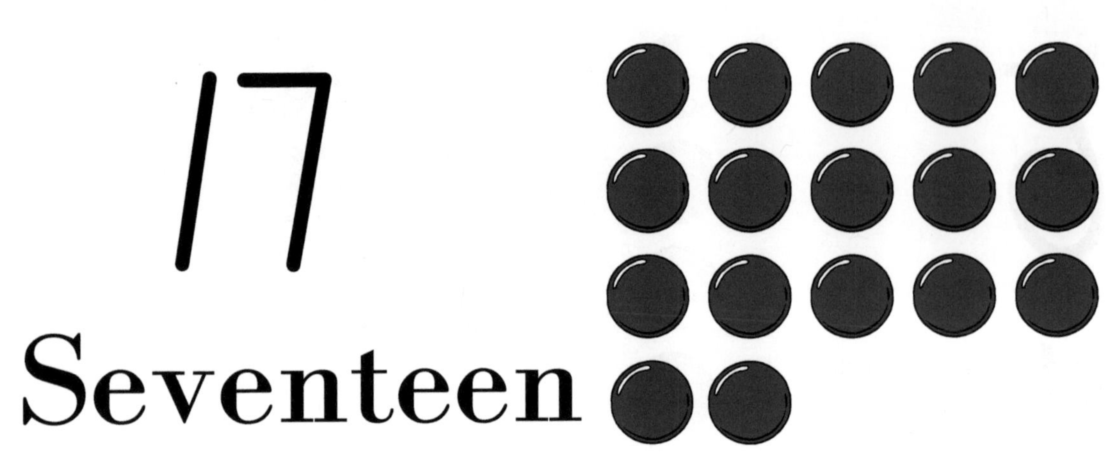

SAY, TRACE AND WRITE

17 17 17 17 17

17

17

17

17

18

Eighteen

SAY, TRACE AND WRITE

18 18 18 18 18

18

18

18

18

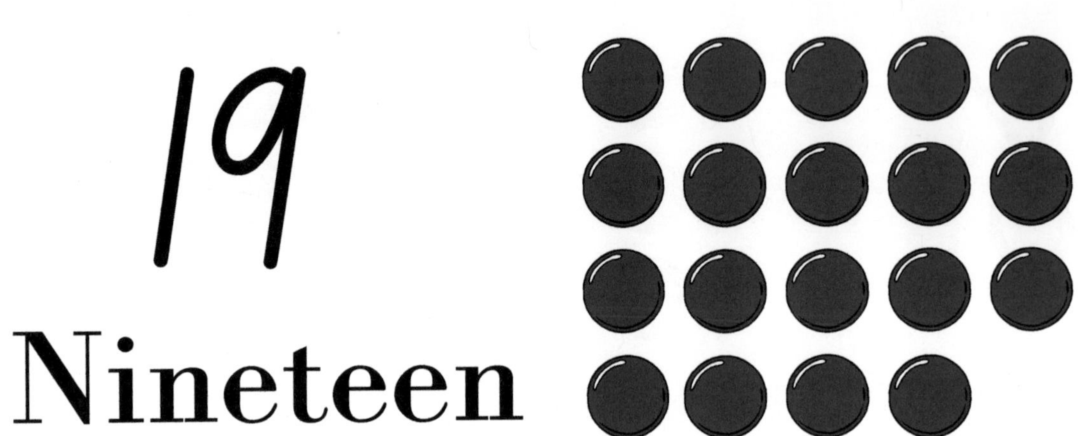

SAY, TRACE AND WRITE

19 19 19 19 19

19

19

19

19

20

Twenty

SAY, TRACE AND WRITE

20 20 20 20 20

20

20

20

20

WRITE THE NUMBERS FROM 16 TO 20

16					
17					
18					
19					
20					

COUNT AND WRITE THE CORRECT NUMBER

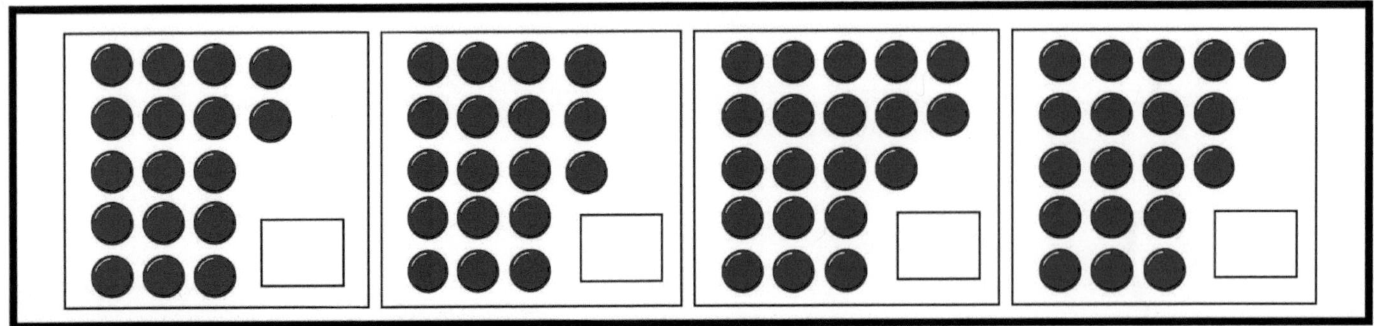

A NEW LOOK AT NUMBERS

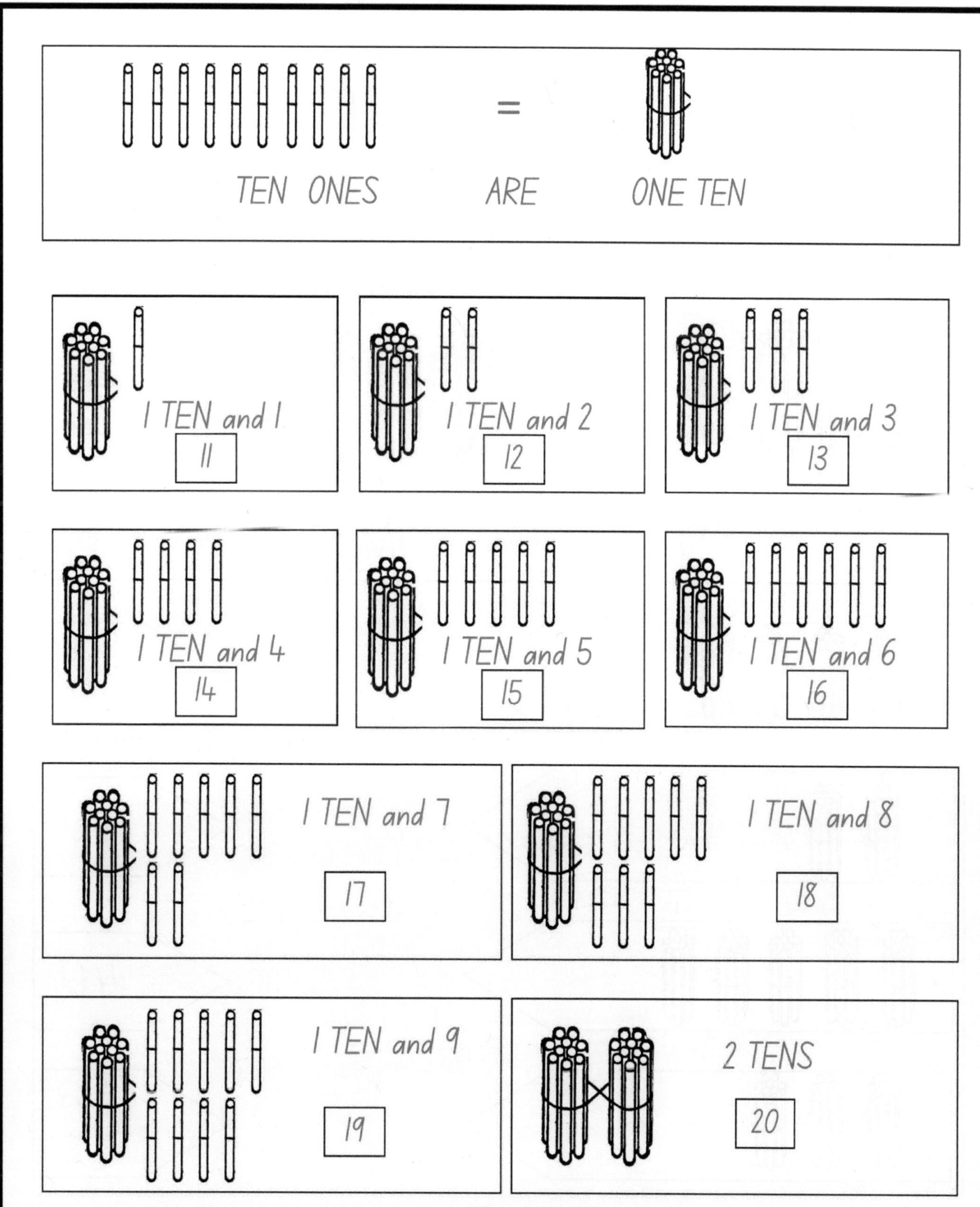

COUNTING BY TENS

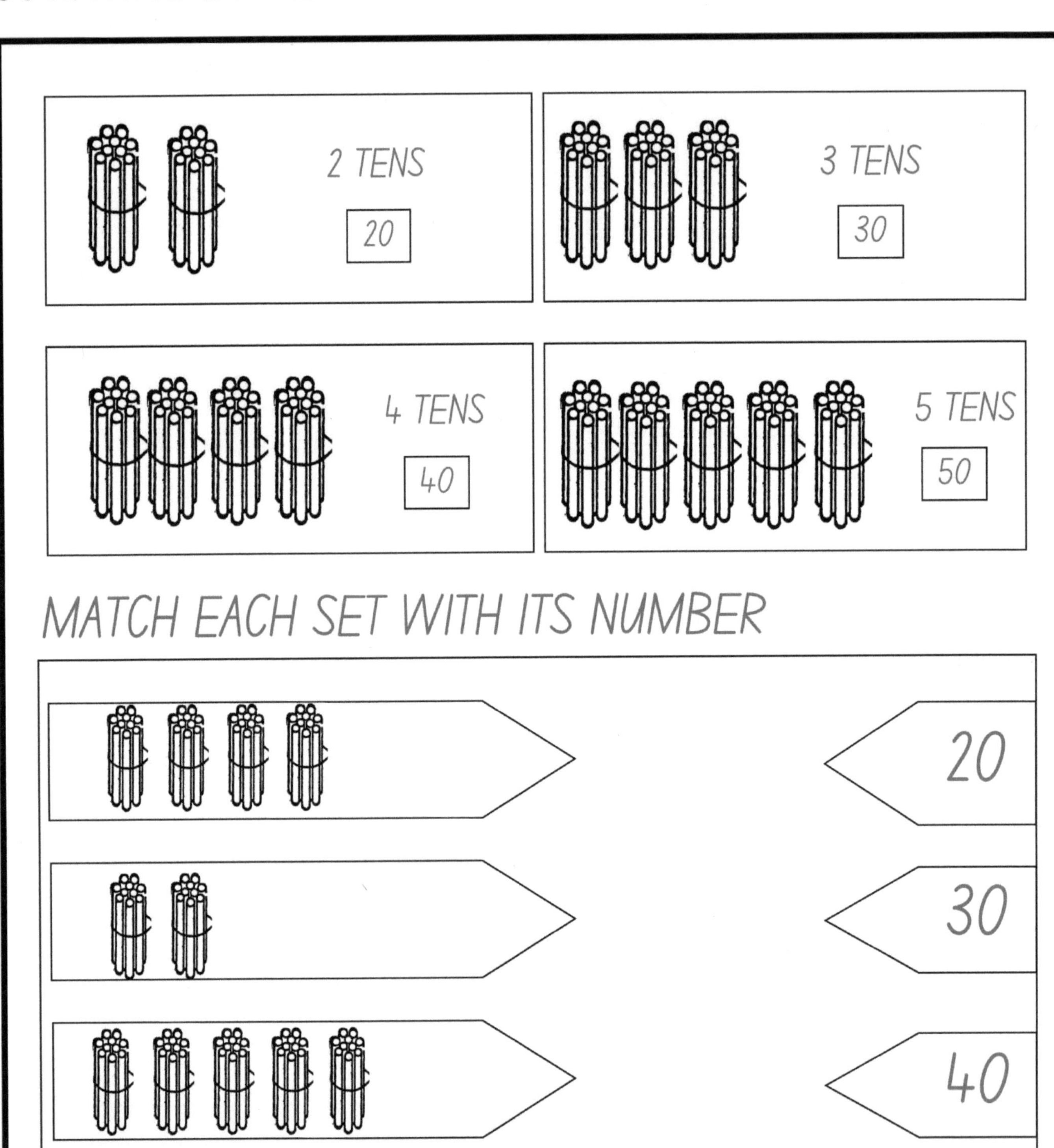

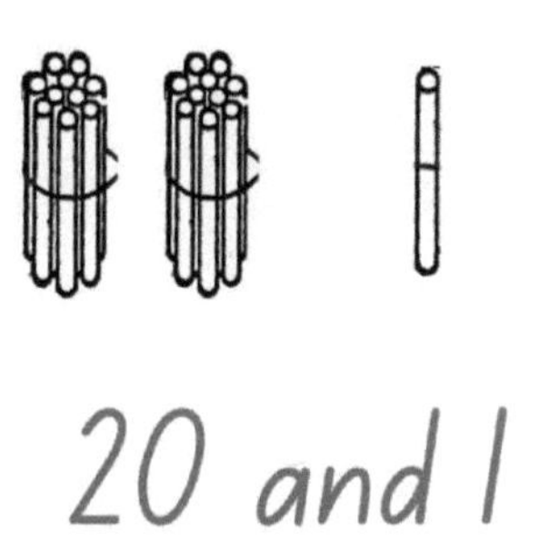

20 and 1

21

Twenty One

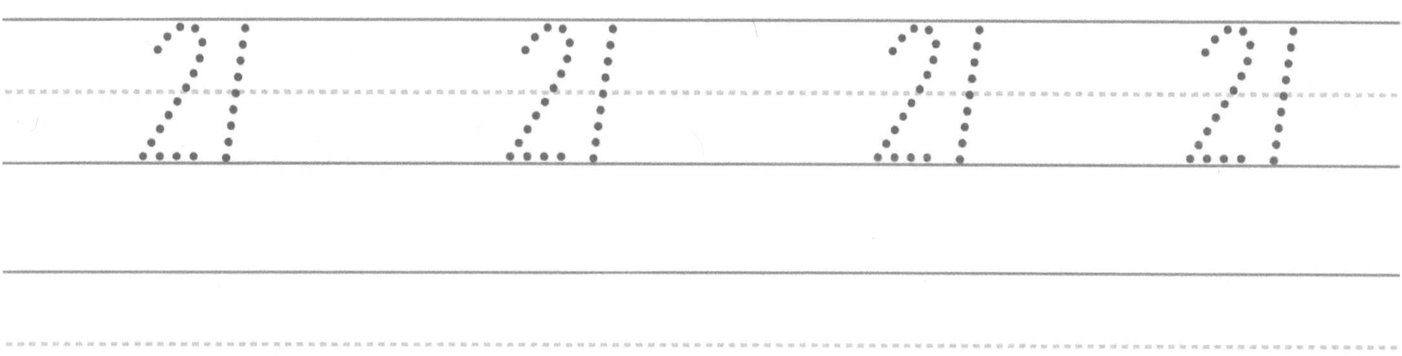

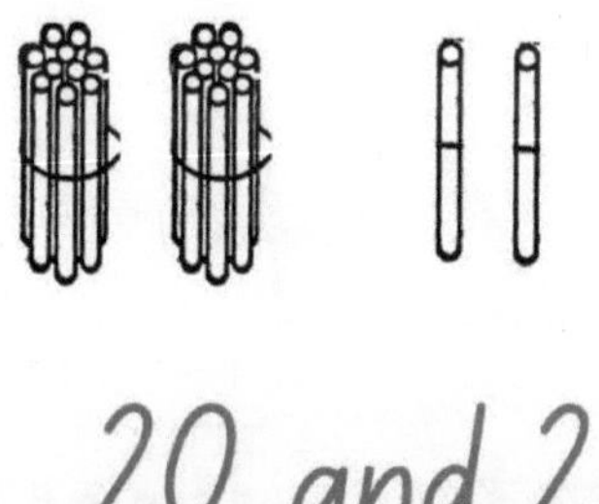

20 and 2

22

Twenty Two

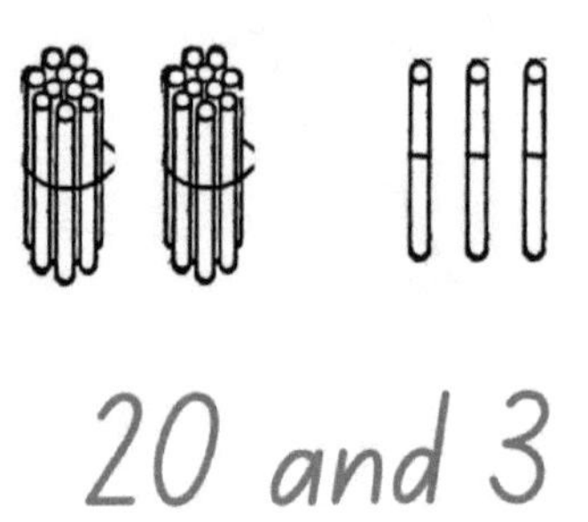

20 and 3

23

Twenty Three

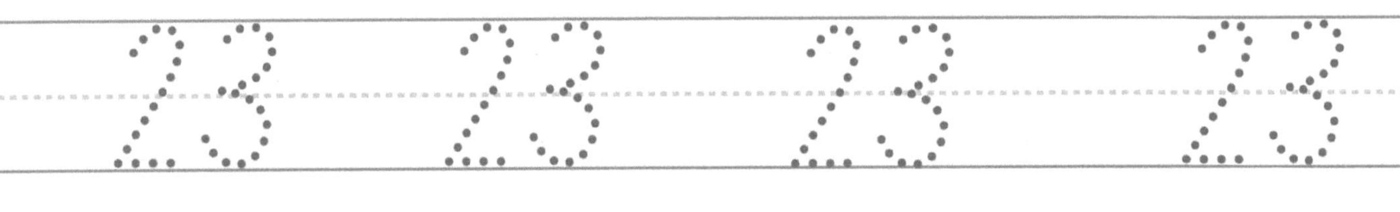

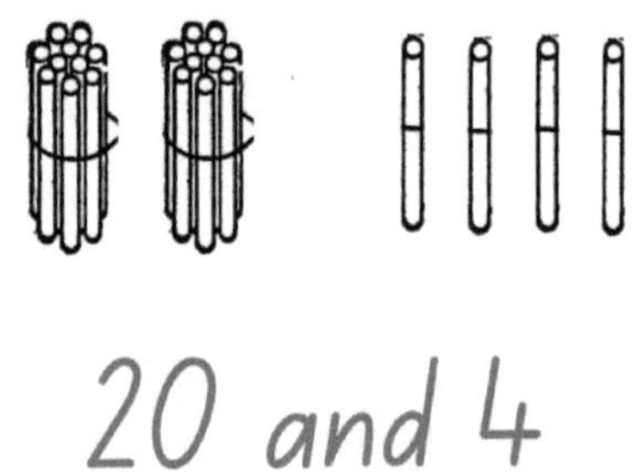

20 and 4

24

Twenty Four

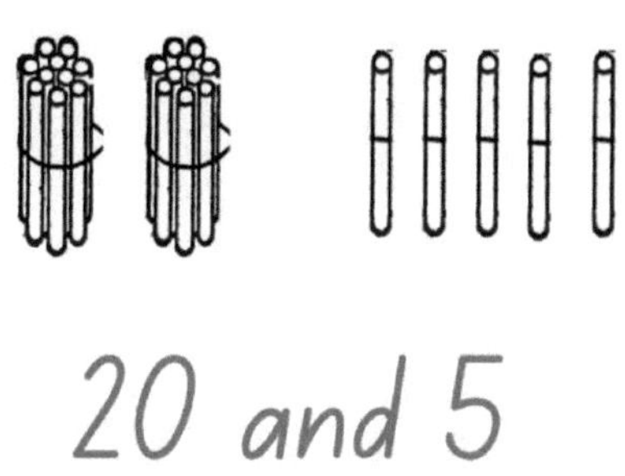

20 and 5

25

Twenty Five

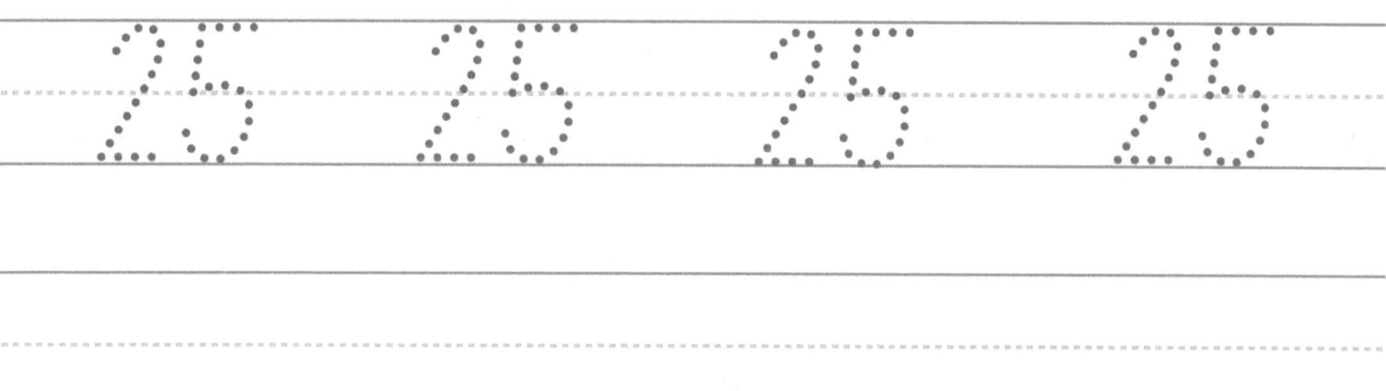

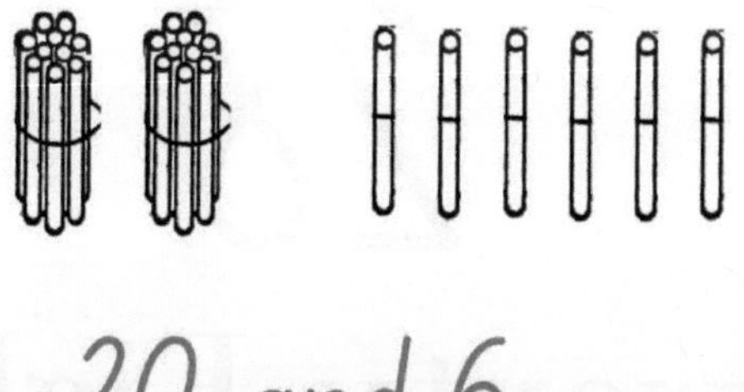

20 and 6

26

Twenty Six

25 25 25 25

26 26 26 26

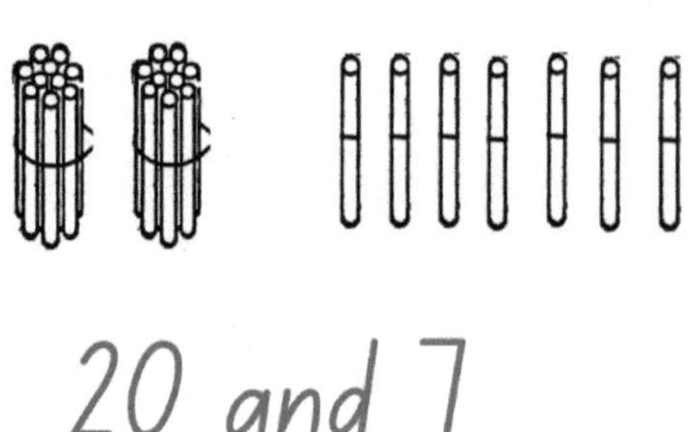

27

20 and 7

Twenty Seven

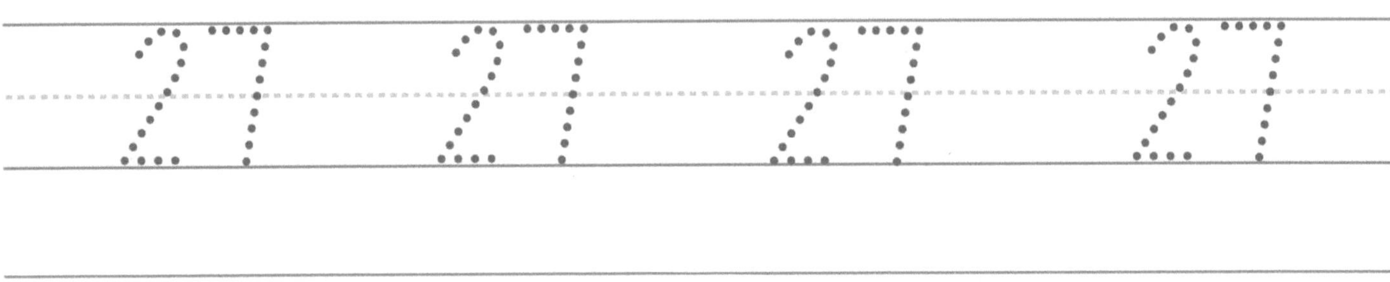

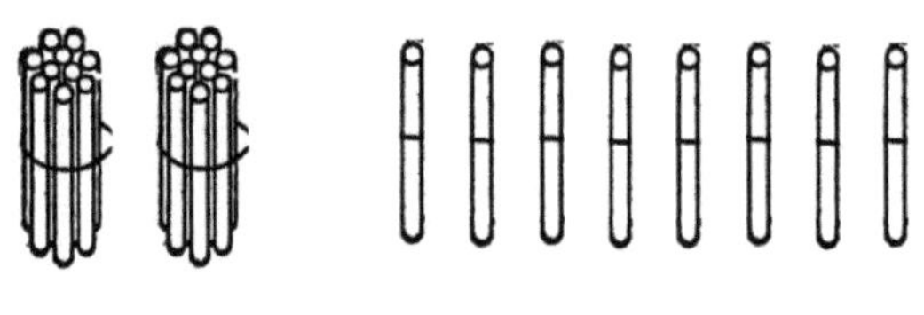

28

20 and 8

Twenty Eight

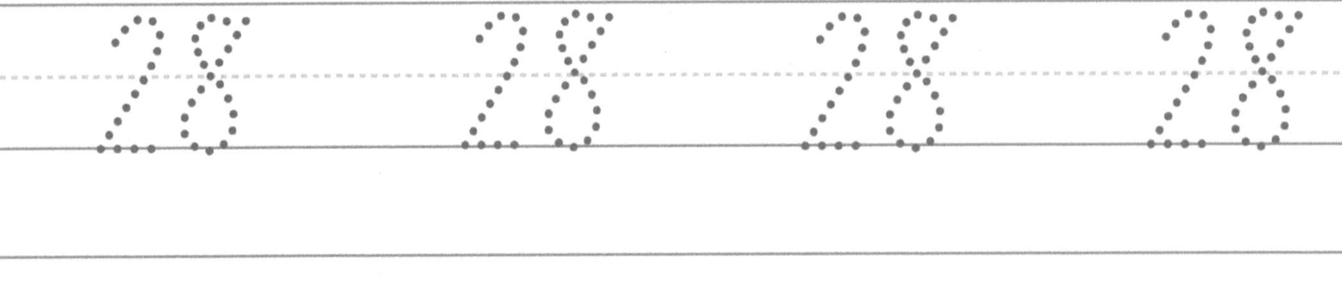

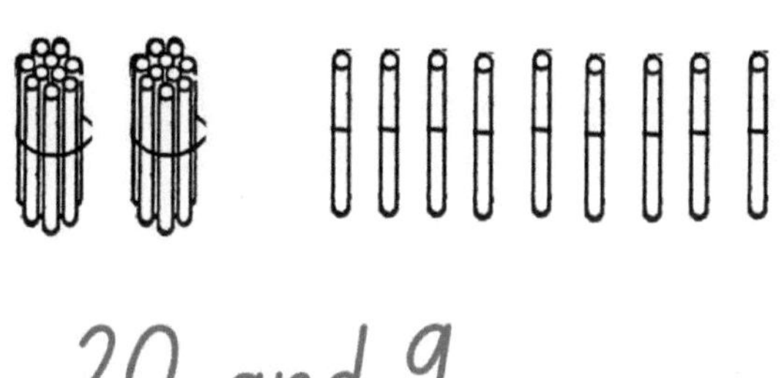

29

20 and 9

Twenty Nine

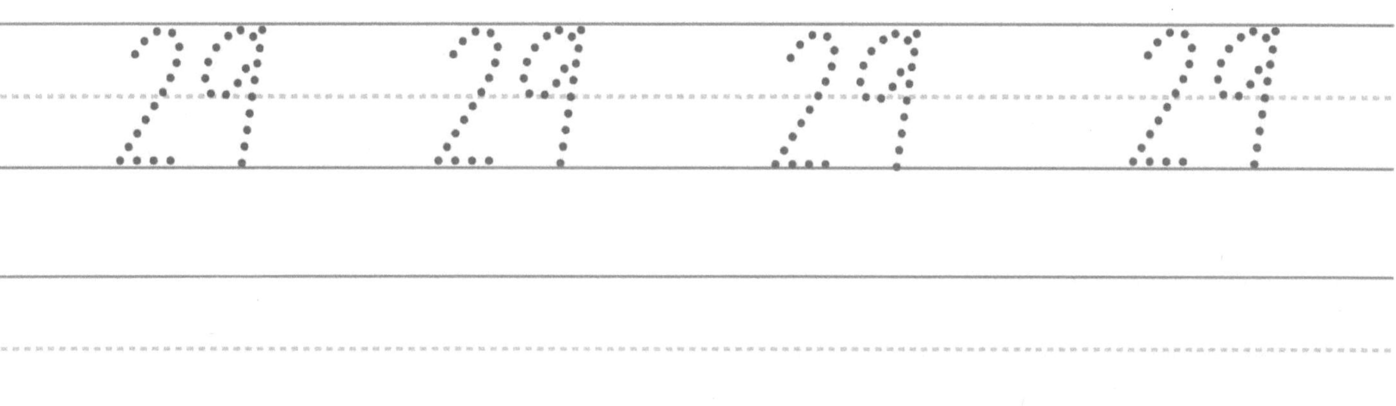

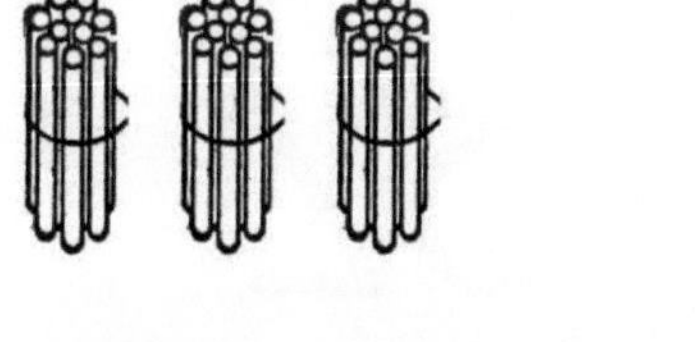

30

20 and 10 (3 Tens)

Thirty

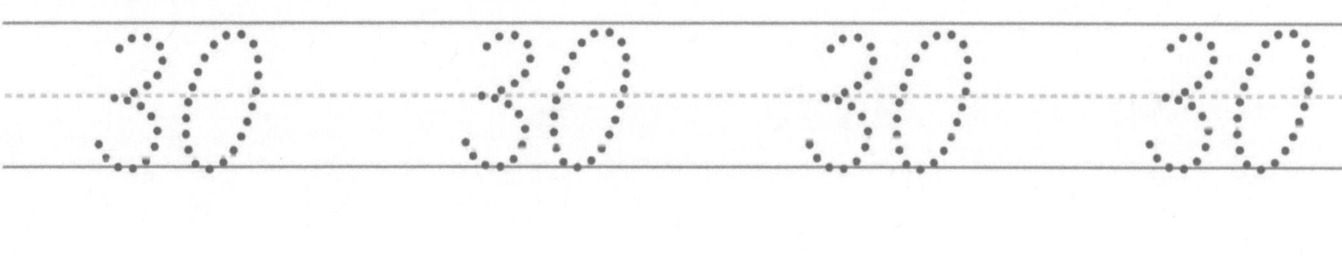

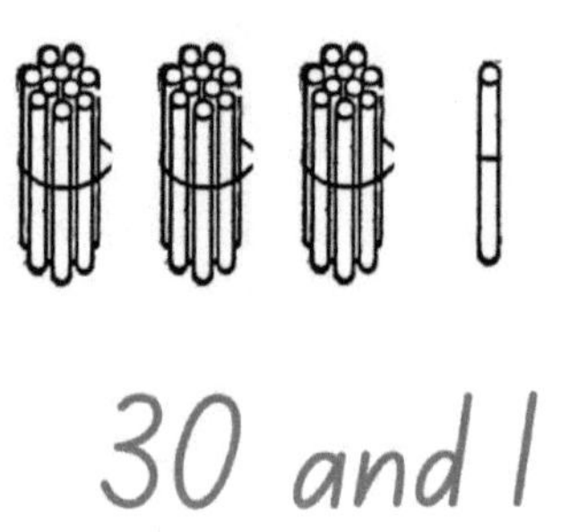

30 and 1

31

Thirty One

31 31 31 31

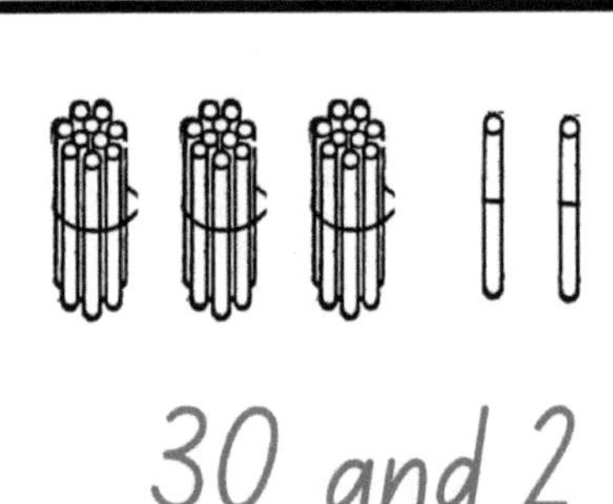

30 and 2

32

Thirty Two

32 32 32 32

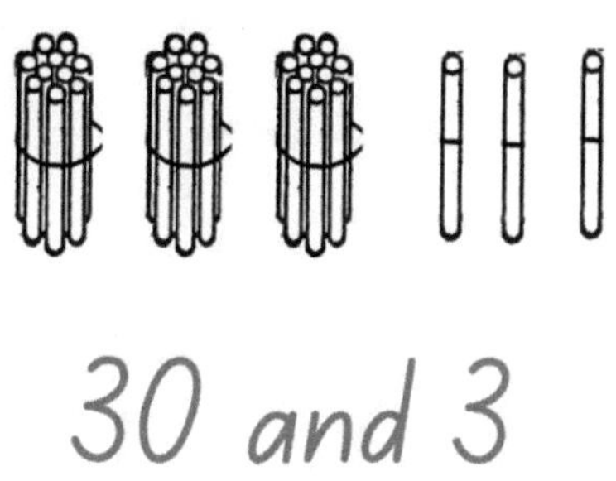

30 and 3

33

Thirty Three

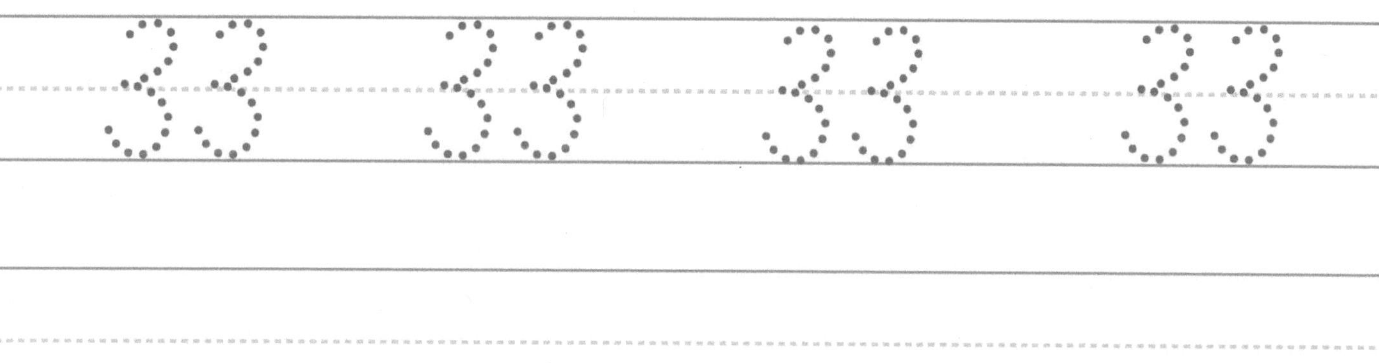

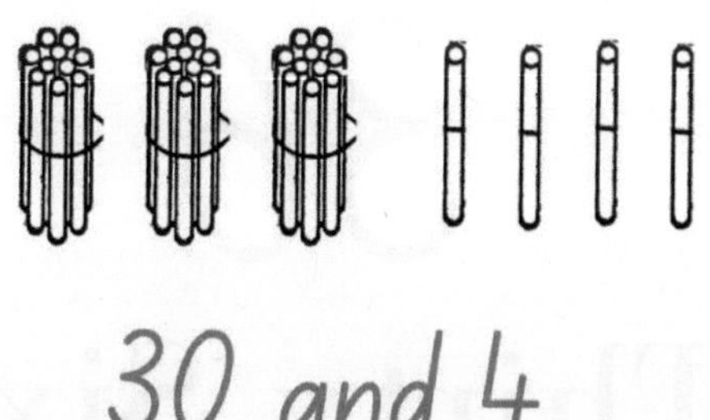

30 and 4

34

Thirty Four

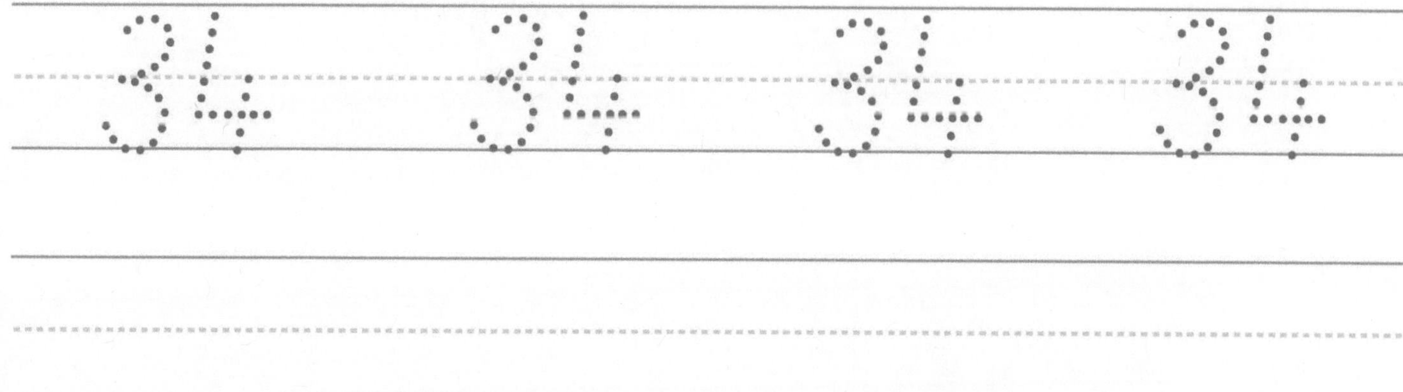

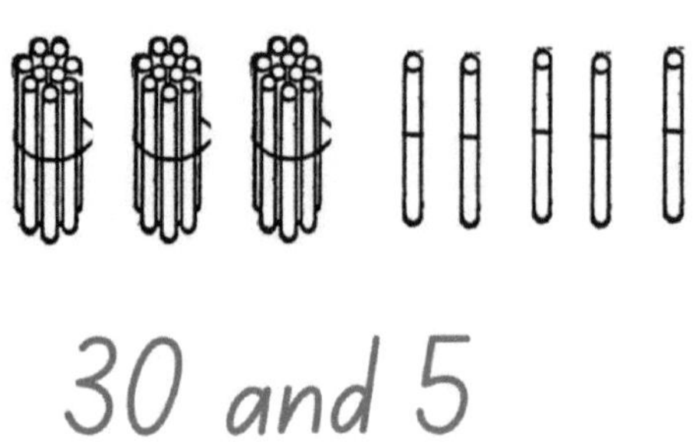

30 and 5

35

Thirty Five

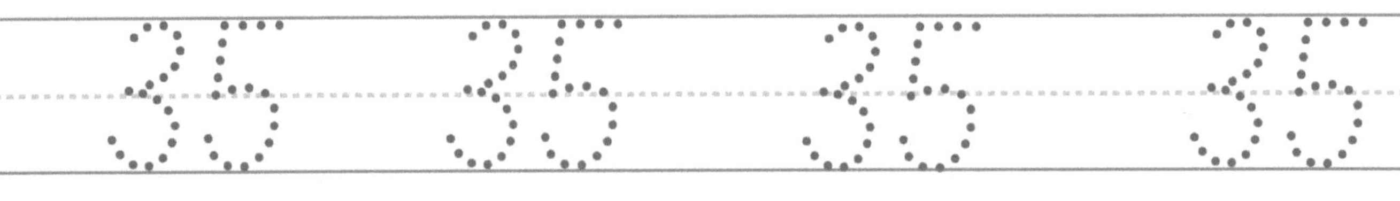

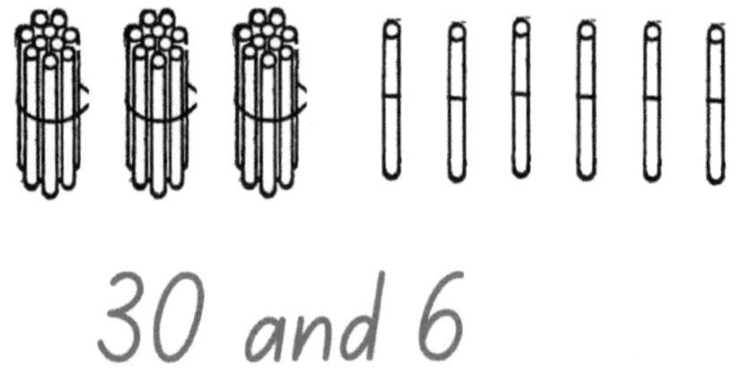

30 and 6

36

Thirty Six

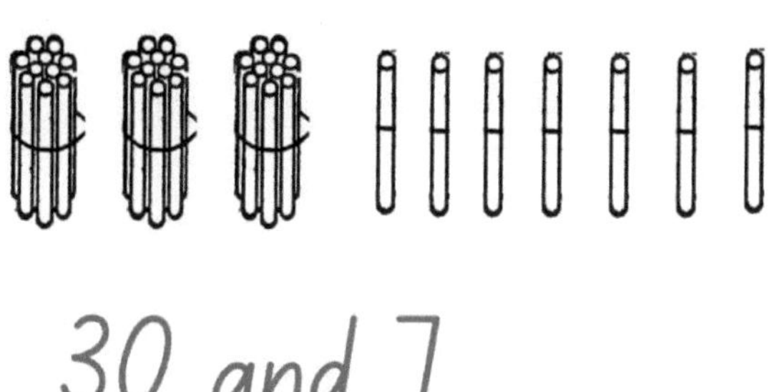

37

30 and 7

Thirty Seven

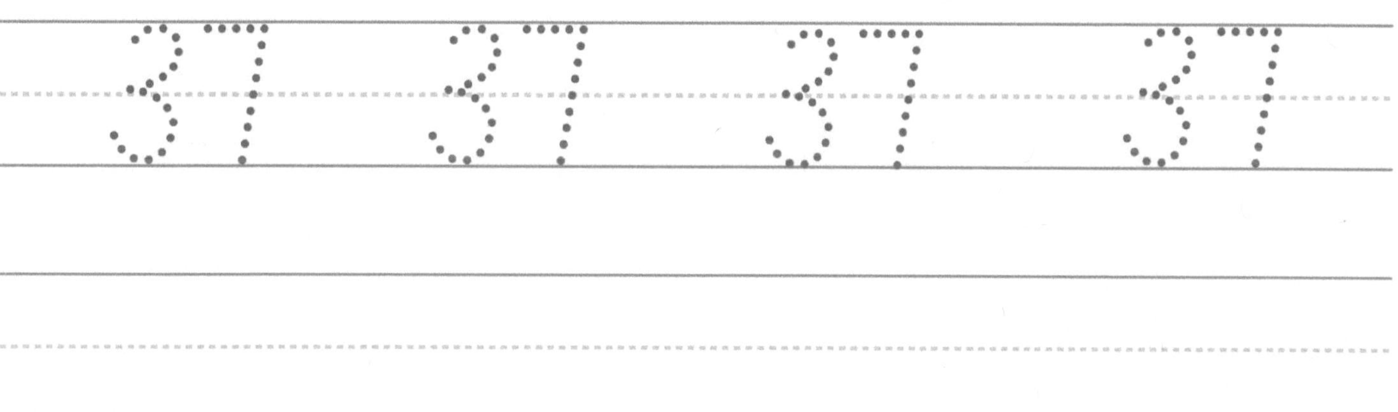

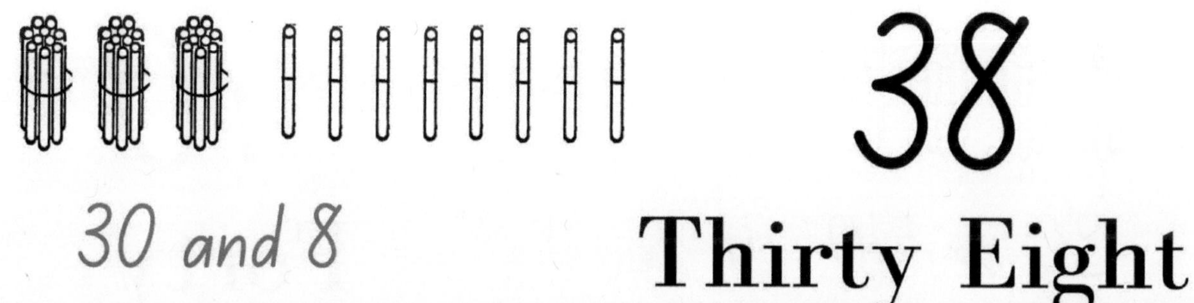

38

30 and 8

Thirty Eight

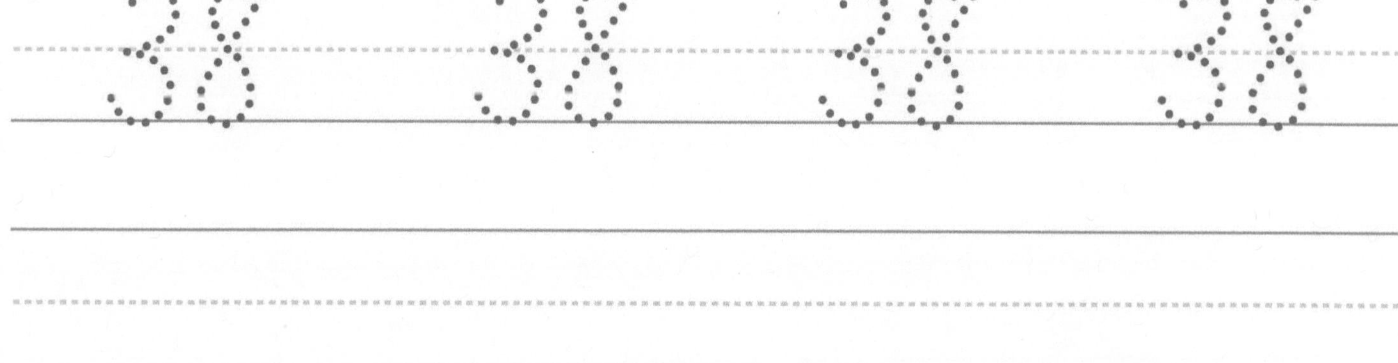

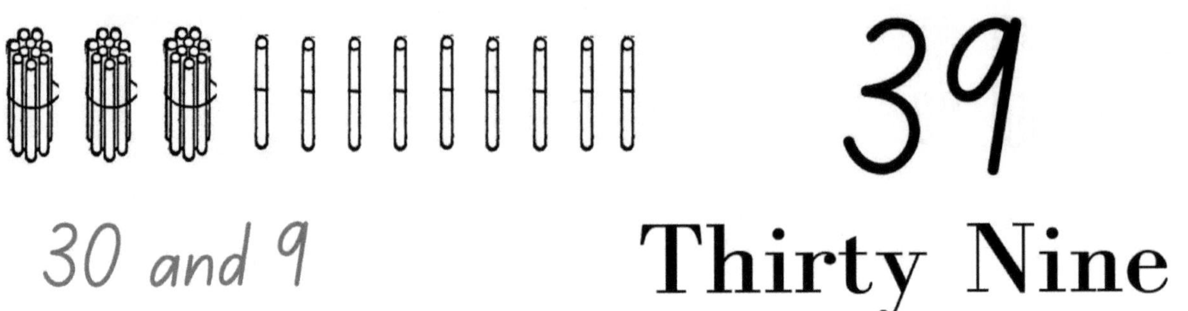

39

30 and 9

Thirty Nine

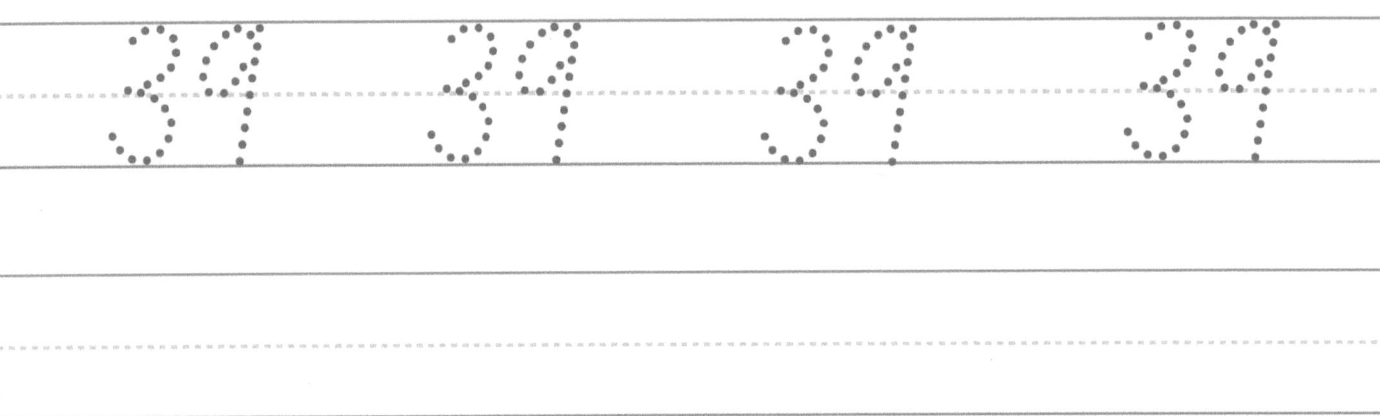

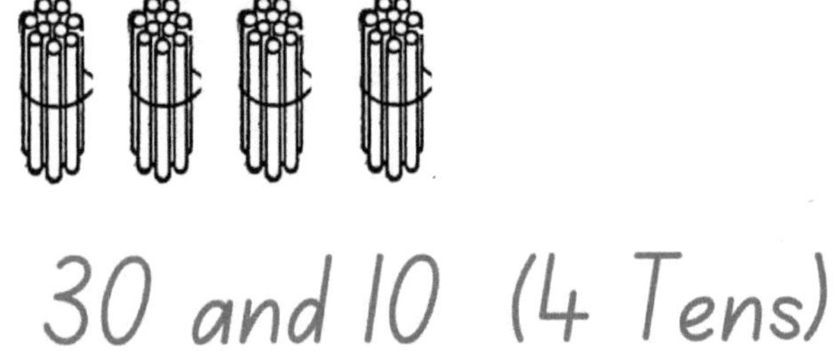

40

30 and 10 (4 Tens)

Forty

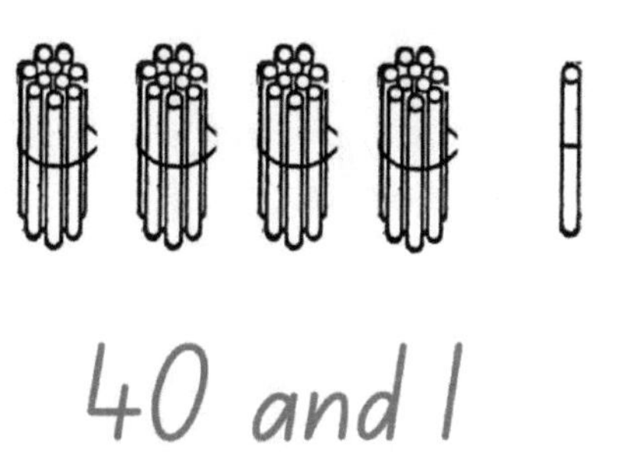

41

40 and 1

Forty One

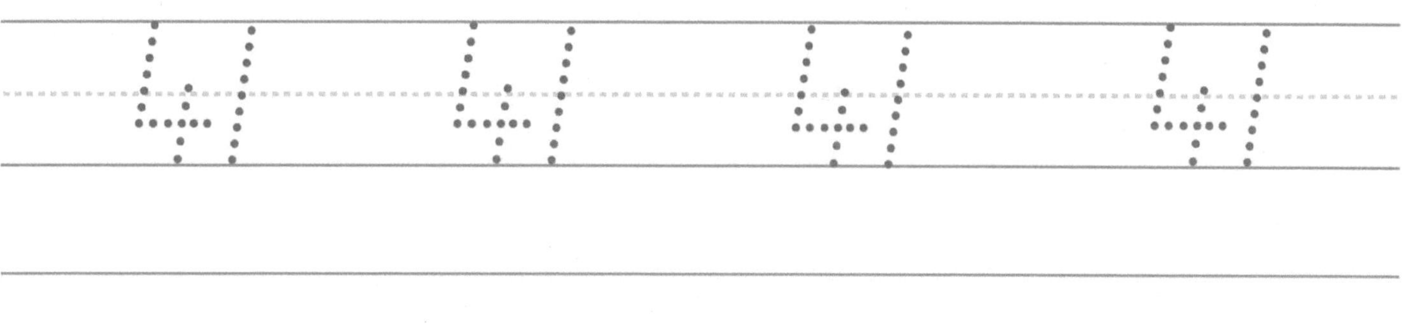

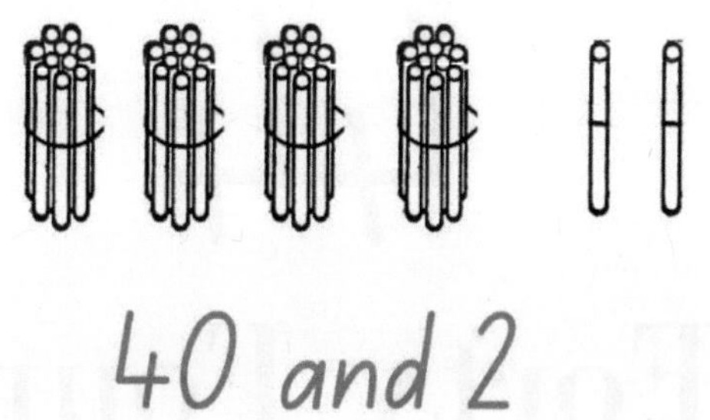

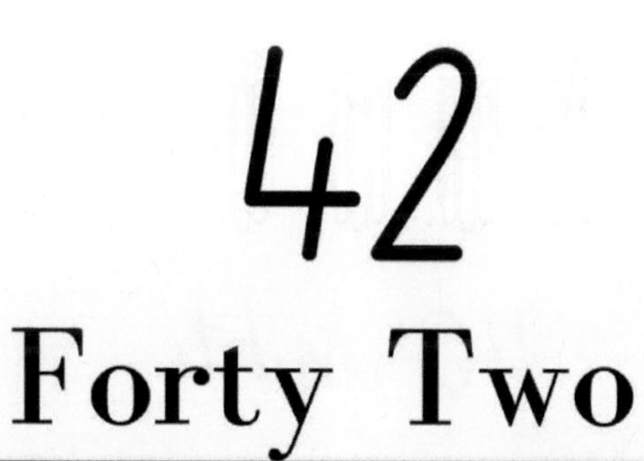

42

40 and 2

Forty Two

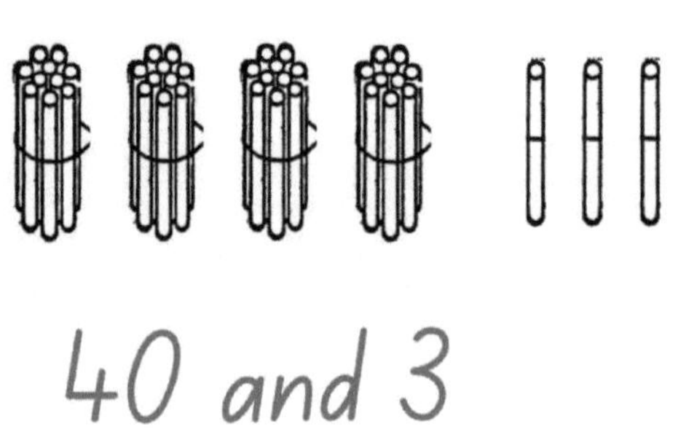

40 and 3

43

Forty Three

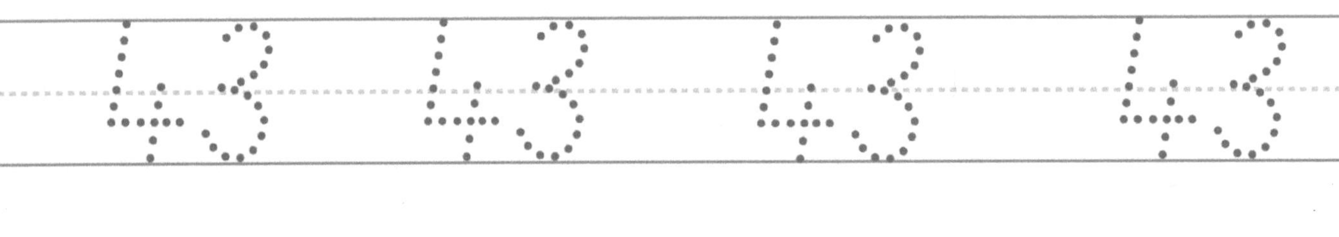

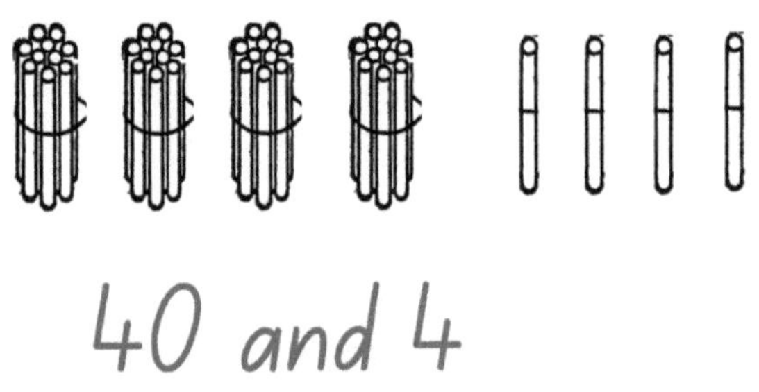

40 and 4

44

Forty Four

44 44 44 44

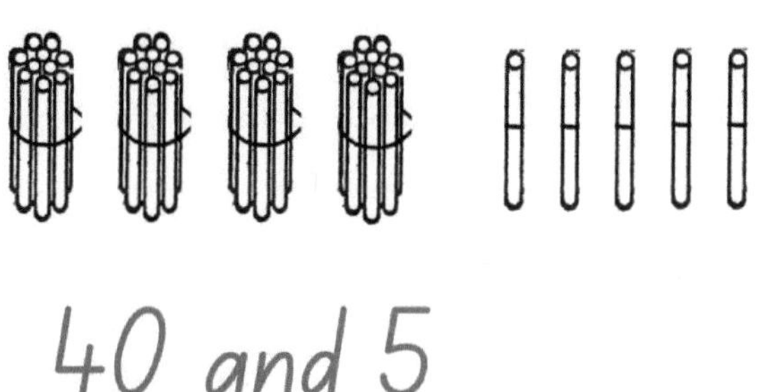

40 and 5

45

Forty Five

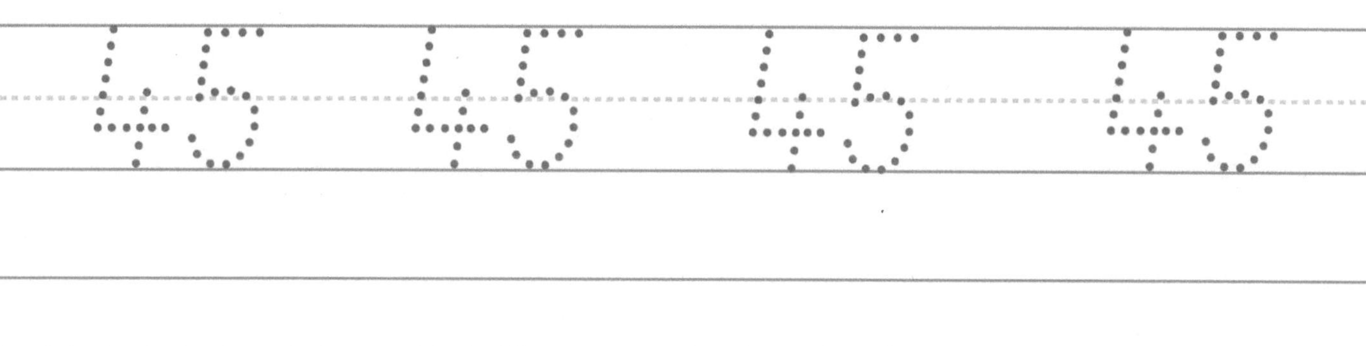

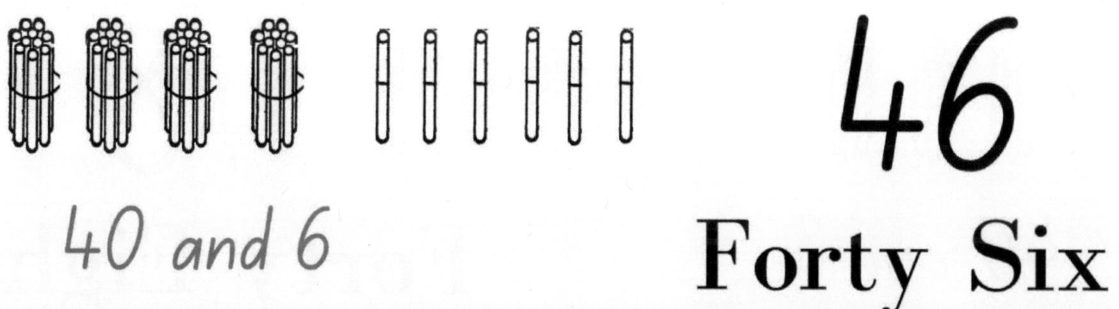

40 and 6

46

Forty Six

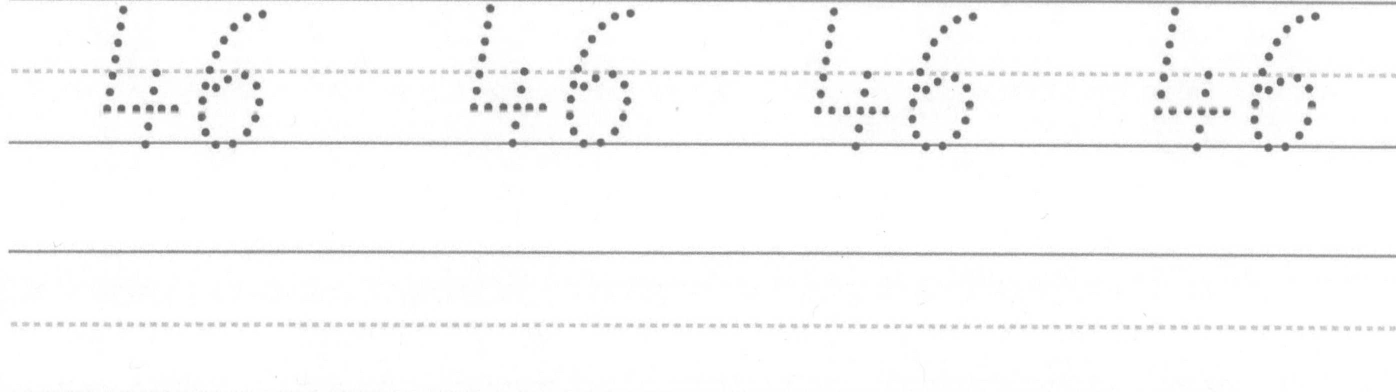

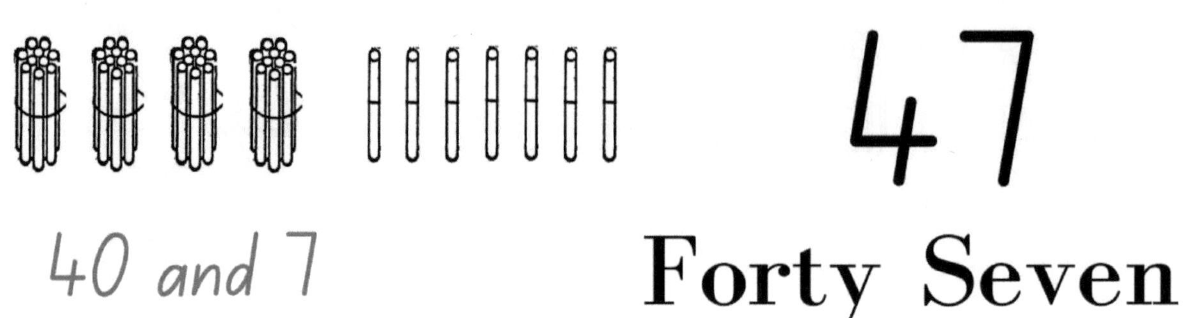

40 and 7

Forty Seven

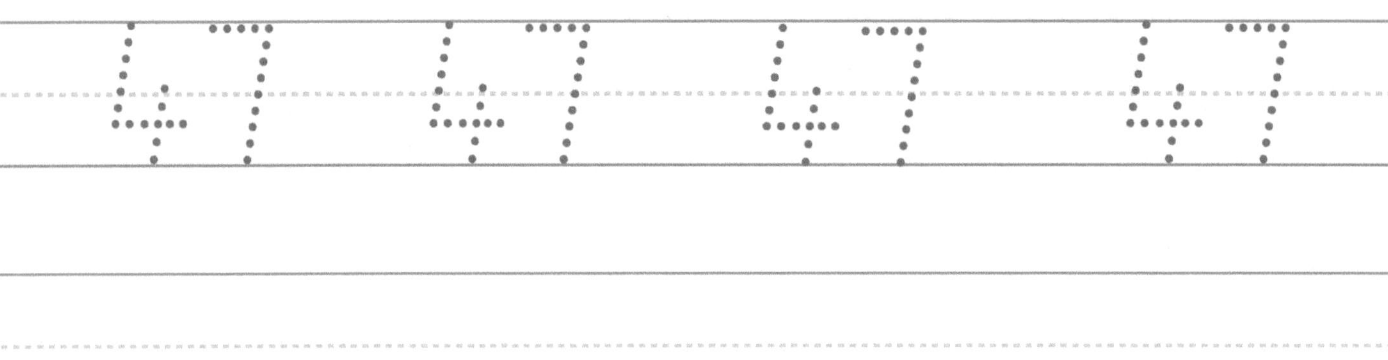

48

40 and 8

Forty Eight

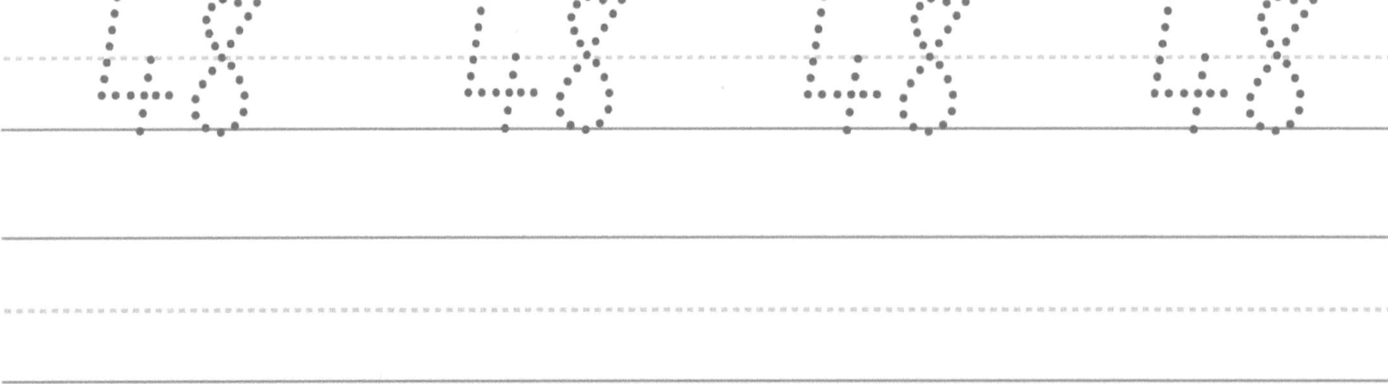

49

40 and 9

Forty Nine

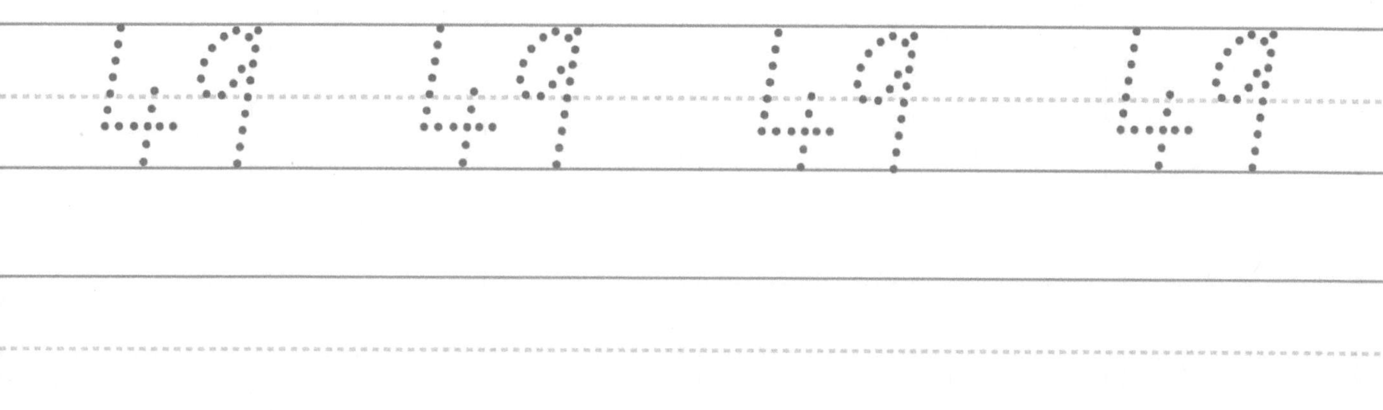

50

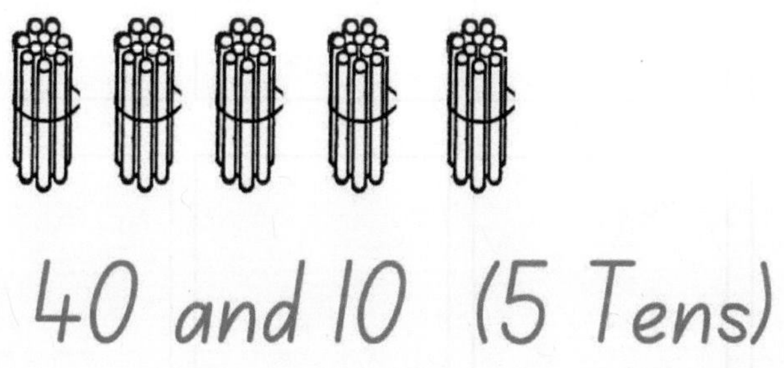

40 and 10 (5 Tens)

Fifty

WRITE THE NUMBERS FROM 21 TO 27

21					
22					
23					
24					
25					
26					
27					

WRITE THE NUMBERS FROM 28 TO 34

28					
29					
30					
31					
32					
33					
34					

WRITE THE NUMBERS FROM 35 TO 41

35					
36					
37					
38					
39					
40					
41					

WRITE THE NUMBERS FROM 42 TO 48

42					
43					
44					
45					
46					
47					
48					

WRITE THE NUMBERS FROM 49 AND 50

49					
50					

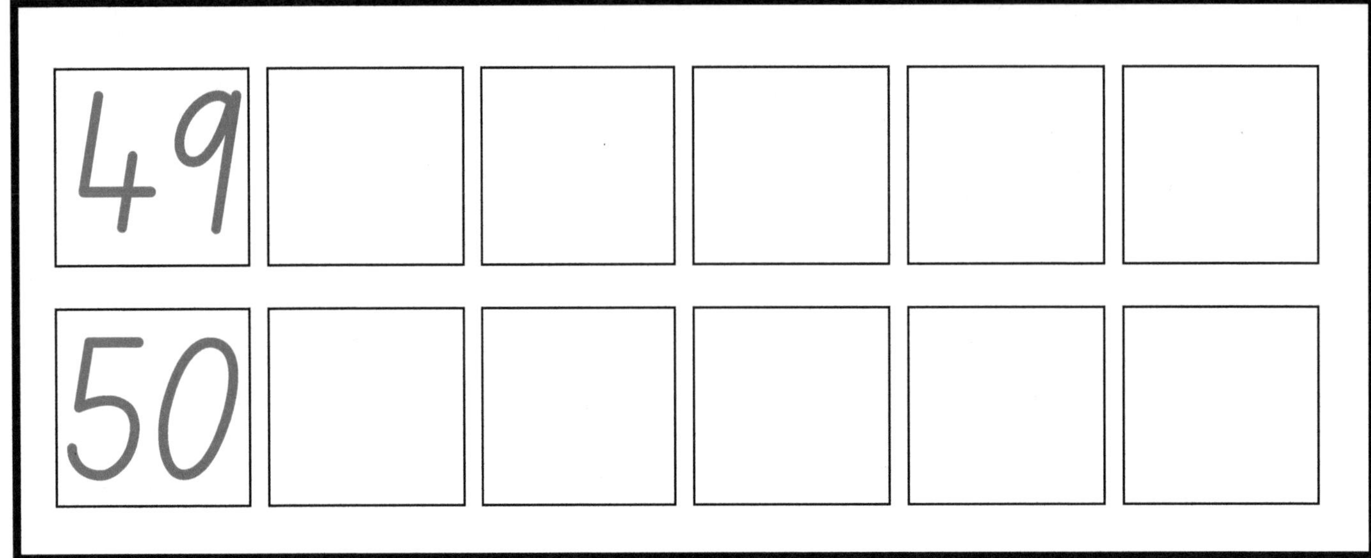

WRITE THE MISSING NUMBERS

2 __	5 __	9 __
12 __	15 __	19 __
__ 2	__ 27	__ 30
__ 33	__ 36	__ 40
42 __ 44	45 __ 47	__ 49 __

Printed by Libri Plureos GmbH in Hamburg,
Germany